Stanley
The Snack Snatcher

Lemi-Ola Erinkitola

Illustrated by Yuffie Yuliana

ISBN: 0989993345
ISBN-13: 978-0-9899933-4-0

For
Mom, Dad, Gigi,
Jai and Foluke

Stanley Stevens sprinted into the school cafeteria

where Susan was sitting.

"Stop! Stanley, Stop! Stop stealing my snacks!" said Susan.

"This is your sixth snatch of the school year!"

Munch! Munch! Munch!

Sadly, Susan sighed and sobbed as Stanley

slobbered,

slurped, and

snatched Susan's sweet snacks.

Stanley smiled and sang as he skipped away.

Susan smirked, scratched her scalp, and schemed up a plan.

"Stanley the Snack Snatcher will stop someday!" said Susan.

Susan had a strategy.

"A sour snack should stop Stanley from stealing."

The next day, she snuck a sour snack into her lunch sack.

Surprise! Stanley scampered into the cafeteria again and

snatched the sour snack.

Munch! Munch! Munch!

Sadly, Susan sighed and sobbed as Stanley

slobbered,

slurped, and

stole Susan's entire sour snack.

Susan had a second strategy.

"A spicy snack should stop Stanley from stealing," said Susan.

The next day, she snuck a spicy snack into her lunch sack.

Swiftly, Stanley came into the cafeteria and

snatched the spicy snack.

Sizzle! Sizzle! Sizzle!

Munch! Munch! Munch!

Susan sighed and sobbed as Stanley the Snack Snatcher

slobbered,

slurped, and

stole Susan's spicy snack.

Susan had a third strategy, and this time she hoped to stop

the snack snatcher finally.

"A sticky snack should stop Stanley from stealing," said Susan.

The next day, she snuck a sticky snack into her lunch sack.

Stanley sprang into the cafeteria and snatched the sticky snack.

Soon, Stanley was silent.

Stanley's mouth was stuck!

Stanley the Snack Snatcher stammered and spluttered

as he slipped on the snack.

Susan was startled!

The next school day, Stanley said to Susan

"Sorry for stealing your snacks."

"Sorry too for the sour, spicy and sticky snacks," said Susan.

"Can we be friends now?" Stanley asked.

"Yes, we can be friends" Susan replied.

Susan and Stanley smiled as they slurped and smacked on their own sweet and savory snacks.

The End

www.ingramcontent.com/pod-product-compliance
Lightning Source LLC
Chambersburg PA
CBHW041240040426
42445CB00004B/96